SURVIVAL GUIDE TO

Edible
Insects

FRED DEMARA

PALADIN PRESS • BOULDER, COLORADO

Also by Fred Demara:
Eating on the Run: Survival Foraging for Plants, Grasses, Nuts, and Berries

Survival Guide to Edible Insects
by Fred Demara
Copyright © 2013 by Fred Demara

ISBN 13: 978-1-61004-870-5
Printed in the United States of America

Published by Paladin Press, a division of
Paladin Enterprises, Inc.
Gunbarrel Tech Center
7077 Winchester Circle
Boulder, Colorado 80301 USA, +1.303.443.7250

Direct inquiries and/or orders to the above address.

PALADIN, PALADIN PRESS, and the "horse head" design
are trademarks belonging to Paladin Enterprises and
registered in United States Patent and Trademark Office.

Neither the author nor the publisher assumes
any responsibility for the use or misuse of
information contained in this book.

Visit our website at www.paladin-press.com

CONTENTS

Introduction 1

Earthworms 7

Snails and Slugs 10

Butterflies and Moths 12

      Pandora Moth Larvae 12

      Armyworms (Miller Moths) 14

      Corn Borers 16

      Tomato Hornworms and Tobacco Hornworms 17

Grasshoppers (Locusts), Crickets, and Katydids 19

Cicadas and Aphids 26

Ants, Bees, and Wasps 30

      Ants 30

      Bees 31

      Wasps 32

Termites 34

Beetles 36

      June Bugs 36

      Western Corn Rootworm 37

Giant Water Bug 39

"American" Cockroach 41

Woodlice. 43

Desert Centipede 46

Dragonfly (Common Green Darner) 48

Shore Flies 49

Houseflies. 51

Spiders and Scorpions 53

Microbes, Toxins, or Allergens. 55

INTRODUCTION
The Nutritious World of Invertebrates

Man's travels and activities have had a marked, if not always beneficial, impact on the flora and fauna of this planet. As do most animal species, we roam and graze, ever curious of what is beyond the horizon. Just in case what is beyond the horizon might not include some of our favored foods, we are inclined to take them along as we explore, or redistribute back to the Old Country the desirable things we find in new places. And for better or worse, we also usually redistribute unknown hitchhikers during our running to and fro.

Because of this, nearly every venue has been affected by "invasive" species of plant and animal life, brought there by man's activities. Some have competed very well, at the expense of the "native" species. Some are a pure nuisance, but many are useful and even edible.

For the purpose of finding emergency food, it makes no difference whether the fauna has grown here since before recorded time, was brought here by migrating populations as a crop, or was an "oops" that sneaked in, as did the Formosan termite, roly-poly, and various snails. When your meal is where you find it, then it's all good. Thus, although this volume is primarily a guide for survival foraging on the North American continent, because many of the invertebrates available may be imports or species naturally of universal distribution, I hope that this wide distribution from whatever cause will extend its geographic usefulness.

Various invertebrates, from those who creep to those who fly, have always been a prime protein source for the domestic stock we in turn raise for our own needs, especially fish and fowl. Particularly in a remote survival situation, however, we can readily cut out the middleman and eat these various and valuable invertebrates ourselves. We already pay a good price to do it with those deemed "marketable," such as escargot and various shellfish.

Earlier civilizations worldwide used this bounty as a primary protein source—and as this is being written, all over the world folks are sitting down to enjoy a hearty repast of small things that were slow enough to be caught. The premise of this work is that if it's what's there, and you prepare it right, then, hey: "It's what's for dinner!"

GUESS WHO'S CRAWLING TO DINNER?

In Western civilization, particularly the American branch, we have a well-developed antipathy for any animal food that does not look like a chicken, cow, or salmon. "Bugs" in particular are traditionally regarded as vermin and not nutrition, because although mostly not harmful in themselves, historically some have been vectors of disease. In addition to those diseases with which they don't inoculate you directly, some insects will carry other diseases from old source to new victim on their hairy little feet and through their disgusting habit of eating feces and carrion then regurgitating in the egg salad at the Fourth of July picnic. But there is far more to the invertebrate realm than ticks, flies, fleas, and mosquitoes. As many as 10,000,000 species exist of insects alone, with only about a million having been classified. Among those, the bad actors are well known but taint the reputation of the whole class.

"Bugs" from mollusks and myriad larvae to insects and arachnids have a real public relations problem with cultures that have been raised with the Old Testament health laws—very practical but very restrictive—as the basic tenants of wholesomeness. A man in a starvation situation may have to either lower his standards or broaden his horizons (depending on your point of view) to keep fueled. To sustain life, if you don't have the food you love, then you'd better learn to love the food you have. It's that simple.

ENLIGHTENED ENTOMOPHAGY

The term *entomophagy* comes from the Greek *entomos* (insect[ed]) and *phăgein* (to eat) and refers to the consumption of insects as food. As applied more broadly, it refers to eating other crustaceans as well, plus mollusks, as long as they are not found in the market, as are the socially accepted crabs, oysters, and shrimp.

But there is very good news: a large segment of the Earth's population is way ahead of the West when it comes to putting nutrition ahead of esthetics, and much of their advantage is purely in their perception. Why would we pay premium prices for crab and run from a spider? Why would we excitedly put on a special bib for a feast of crayfish but never do more than stomp on a cricket? Or take 10 minutes with wrinkled brow and pursed lips deciding on the best wine to go with that plate of escargot and go "eeewww" when we see slime trails of slugs across our back porch or over our nylon tent? Why was the North American practice of harvesting grasshoppers by burning meadows to simultaneously remove their wings and roast them regarded as truly aboriginal, but when John the Baptist lived on locusts and wild honey he was the ultimate survivorman?

Even a rhetorical question deserves an answer, and in this case it is simple and obvious: our Western distaste and reluctance for bugs as food is because we have consistently confused the critter, which very seldom has any harmful effect as food, with the deadly microbes that may be carried by his distant cousin.

As this is written, half a day's drive from my place was the site last year of one of the most deadly foodborne disease outbreaks in a generation, a listeriosis eruption that infected 146 and killed 32 across the United States, and the carrier was not insects or maggots but simply (*ta daa!*) cantaloupe. Within sight of here are some of the most pristine mountain waters on our continent, and those pristine mountain waters are high-risk areas for giardia outbreaks. Are we to avoid any possible carrier of a disease—or the microbes that produce the disease itself? We must not confuse the disease with a possible carrier. I personally like water and cantaloupe, and folks all over the planet like insects and grubs and squishy things. We might benefit from their better discernment. Western avoidance of entomophagy coexists with the consumption of other invertebrates, such as crustaceans and mollusks, and is based solely on culture, not taste or food value.

Boiling your water or roasting your bugs isn't that big a deal: you don't eat a lot of raw chicken and pork, do you? It is only one's background, certainly not logic, that makes it acceptable to eat raw oysters or steak tartare, both of which can carry either serious gastrointestinal diseases or parasites, but not to eat well-cooked grasshoppers. Although a bottle of hot sauce and a handful of lively crickets is a popular snack in southern Mexico, your preference might be to cook it all—but to eat it all if it is nutritious, and tasty. In any case, cooking, particularly roasting of hard-shelled insects, tends overall to improve the taste.

EAT A BUG? NOT ME!

To those who vow to starve before they would "eat a bug," we might question their virginity if they have been eating from the grocery store. According to the U.S. Department of Agriculture, here are some perfectly OK levels of bugs, bug parts, or bug excrement in some typical foods:

- Wheat flour (insect filth): average of up to 150 or more insect fragments per 100 grams
- Frozen broccoli (insects/mites): average of 60 or more aphids and/or thrips and/or mites per 100 grams
- Hops (insects): average of more than 2,500 aphids per 10 grams (that works out to 7,500-plus aphids per ounce of hops)
- Ground thyme (insect filth): average of 925 or more insect fragments per 10 grams
- Ground nutmeg (insect filth): average of 100 or more insect fragments per 10 grams

Considering the lingering toxicity of various chlorinated hydrocarbon or heavy-metal sprays used on food to keep it bug free, I don't mind a few bugs here and there.

Of course, just the same as many plants are inedible or toxic, so are some insects, although the percentages tend to show the prevailing wholesomeness of bugs as opposed to plants. Throughout this study, I'll try to identify the unlikely looking good guys that are more commonly found and that have been proven in long-term human experience as viable food sources.

A MEGA-MENU

There are some 1,462 recorded species of edible insects—probably more since that tally was made—eaten by more than 3,000 ethnic groups. These include 235 species of butterflies and moths; 344 species of beetles; 313 species of ants, bees, and wasps; and 239 species of grasshoppers, crickets, and cockroaches, among others. Other commonly eaten insects are termites, cicadas, and dragonflies. Insects are known to be eaten in 80 percent of the world's nations. According to the Food and Agriculture Organization (FAO) of the United Nations in Rome, some 2,000,000,000 folks worldwide already supplement their diets with insects, or with arachnids such as spiders and scorpions.

A 200-page report issued by the organization in spring 2013 noted that insects are high in protein and minerals and, when farmed, have a relatively low environmental impact. Earthworms and termites do have significant methane emissions, but compared to beef animals they are significantly less for the amount of food they produce. Further, there is scant biomass of any kind that some insect will not eat, and they are more efficient in converting what they eat into something that we can eat than are traditional domestic livestock and fowl, or even fish. By comparison, a typical insect will convert 4.4 pounds of feed into 2.2 pounds of insect mass, whereas a beef animal will require 17.6 pounds of feed to produce 2.2 pounds of meat. Of course, you can also use insects for animal feed and then eat the animal if you prefer, but in this case we are talking about taking a link or two out of the food chain and eating the bug directly. And why not?

At the present, most edible insects are gathered from the wild; what insect farming there is most often is to produce feedstock for other critters for which there is a cash market. Insect farming per se is viewed by the FAO as "one of the many ways to address food and feed security" because "insects are everywhere and they reproduce quickly," and have a "low environmental footprint." The high-quality nutrients insects can provide might be "particularly important as a food supplement for undernourished children," FAO noted.

In spite of the fact a lot of readers would fully expect the U.N. to tell them to go eat worms, it's hard to fault the historical or scientific validity of the premise. The appropriate insects can be a good source not only of protein, but also fats, vitamins, and minerals. For example, crickets are high in calcium, and termites are rich in iron. One hundred grams of giant silkworm moth larvae, already a byproduct of the silk industry, provide 100 percent of the minimum daily requirement for copper, zinc, iron, thiamin, and riboflavin.

These lowly but prolific life forms have served as traditional foods in most cultures of non-European origin and have played an important role in the history of human nutrition not only in western North America, but also in Africa, Asia, and Latin America. Before humans had tools to hunt or farm, insects no doubt represented an important part of their staple diet, for the same reason that we are studying them in a "survival" context here: they are everywhere, and they are easy to catch bare-handed.

Coprolites (fossilized excrement) in caves from the Ozarks to Mexico indicate that various insects and larvae were common food on ancient man's menu. In other locations, ancient entomophagy practices have been passed down to the present like any other family recipe, forming a traditional entomophagy. Insects and their larvae were nutritional staples for Neolithic Americans, especially in the West and, among those who have been left alone, still are. Throughout Central and South America and Asia, myriad insects or their larvae are both staples and delicacies.

In a wilderness situation, gourmet cooking may not be possible, but good nutrition is. Throughout nature, prey species usually outnumber their predators, and it is the same among the insect world, meaning you (as predator) will have thousands upon thousands of delicacies available for the taking.

Let's examine some of the moving protein sources not everybody is aware of, but which have a good history as wholesome human nutrition.

EARTHWORMS
(Order Haplotaxida)

Earthworms are classified into three main categories, based on where they live and what they like to eat. All three happily live together on the same patch of ground, if it supplies at different depths the various foods that each type likes. First are the leaf litter/compost-dwelling worms (epigeic), e.g. *Eisenia fetida,* the "red wigglers" of commerce that, as you can tell from their Latin name, can make an unpleasant smell. Next are the topsoil- or subsoil-dwelling worms (endogeic) that live on rotted plant materials or castings from epigeic worms. Last are the worms that construct permanent deep burrows through which they visit the surface to obtain plant material for food, such as leaves (anecic), e.g., *Lumbricus terrestris.* These are the night crawlers, and they are the most favorable as food. Any or all may be found as "rain worms" after a soaking rain has saturated the topsoil or flooded their burrows. Earthworms do not hybridize, but there are many, many varieties.

One consideration is that you may not want to eat what the worm ate, so they should be purged, and because they (or what they ate) may harbor parasites or other microbes unhealthy to man, they should be cooked. At home, they are commonly washed and put in cornmeal for a day, as you would do clams, and they trade the gritty contents of their gut for cornmeal. Then they are deep fried until crisp, salted, and eaten, or they may be ground and used as hamburger in myriad recipes.

In the wild, you may have to be content to grab the worms by the head and squeeze them empty, like you would a tube of toothpaste, wash them the best you can and then roast them on a twig or a hot

Lumbricus terrestris is a large, reddish worm species native to Europe, but now also widely distributed elsewhere around the world (along with several other lumbricids) due to human introduction. It has become the "night crawler" of North America. Photo: Michael Linnenbach, via Wikipedia.

rock, or in hot sand, until crisp, or add them to a soup or stew. If cooked, their lunch is not toxic, just gritty.

Earthworms have a mild, earthy flavor that reminds me of catfish or bass, without the fishiness. They dry well, if you need to stock up for a trek. The worms are generally boiled before inclusion in any recipe. They may be boiled for as little as 10 minutes, although some earthworm chefs will boil them as many as five separate times for 10 minutes each time. They may be used directly, or they may be placed on a cookie sheet in a 200-degree oven for 15 to 30 minutes. Use whole, chopped, or as a flour. Flour is prepared with a blender.

Worm Stroganoff

Wash earthworms thoroughly and place in boiling water for three minutes. Pour off water and repeat the boiling process twice. Bake on cookie sheet at 350 degrees F for 15 minutes. Roll the worms in flour, brown in butter, and add salt to taste. Add bouillon and simmer for 30 minutes. Sauté onions and mushrooms in butter. Add onions and mushrooms to the worms. Stir in sour cream or yogurt. Serve over rice or noodles. For more protein, serve over steamed ant eggs or steamed termites.

Deep-Fried Earthworms

Finely chop an apple and put in with worms for a day. Chill worms. Roll in flour with paprika, salt, and pepper. Deep-fry until crisp.

Earthworm Burger

Place worms in cornmeal for a day to purge and then boil for 10–15 minutes, drain, and grind. Use as hamburger in patties, meatloaf, and other dishes that include ground meat.

SNAILS AND SLUGS
(Gastropods)

This European grapevine snail (shown below) and its cousin *Helix aspersa* have become naturalized in North America. All snails and slugs are edible and offer the advantage of being very easy to catch. But all wild snails and slugs can carry dangerous parasites, so they must be cooked thoroughly—especially the giant African snail, recently found in Texas and probably coming to an environs near you. Snails and slugs are best not even handled bare-handed until they have been cooked.

Purging for a day or so with wholesome fodder (most any vegetable you would eat) is recommended. Boiling is preferred in the wild or for smaller snails such as these, as it makes the snail easy to remove from its shell. Boiling in vinegar removes the distasteful slime from a slug, which is its protection since it does not have a shell.

Slugs can be a vector for transmission of parasitic nematodes

European grapevine snail. Photo: Jürgen Schoner, via Wikipedia.

Survival Guide to Edible Insects

A common slug, photographed in the San Francisco Bay area. Across North America, slugs are common to moist areas and come in all sizes and colors. Generally regarded as an agricultural pest, these gastropods can be emergency food, if thoroughly cooked to kill any parasites and purged as described. Remember, critters, like you, are what they eat. Photo: Sanjay Acharya, via Wikipedia.

that cause lungworm in various mammals, so they are usually avoided by hedgehogs and other mammals when other food is available. In a few rare cases, humans have contracted parasite-induced meningitis from eating raw slugs. Cook well.

BUTTERFLIES
AND MOTHS
(Order Lepidoptera)

The larvae (caterpillars) of many species of moths (and a few species of butterflies) are used as food. They are a particularly important source of nutrition (protein, fat, vitamins, and minerals) in Africa. In one country alone, the Democratic Republic of Congo (sometimes referred to as Congo-Kinshasa, formerly Zaire), more than 30 species are harvested. Some caterpillars are sold not only in the local village markets but are also shipped by the tons from one country to another. To man, only the larva are palatable, but grizzlies and brown bears fattening for the winter in the Rocky Mountains have favorite feeding spots for congregating armyworm moths (*Spodoptera frugiperda*).

PANDORA MOTH LARVAE

The use of caterpillars as food has been widely reported throughout Native American populations of the North American Great Basin, but the specific identity is known of only two species of moths: the pandora moth, *Coloradia pandora* (family Saturniidae), and the white-lined sphinx moth, *Hyles lineata* (family Sphingidae).

The food use of the pandora moth is well documented in California, and populations in Arizona have been estimated as high as 100,000 adults per hectare. The caterpillars were known as *piagi* (*pe-ag'-gah*) and similar spellings, depending on the tribe (which means "big fat ones, good to eat"), and they were widely traded. Competition among tribes for this resource has at times nearly resulted in wars, as between California's Mono vs. Miwok or Yokut tribes to the

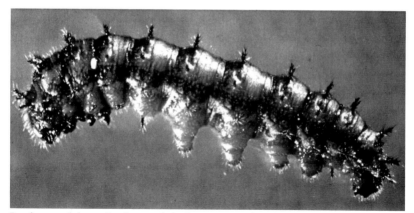

Pandora moth larva. In pinewoods in the summer, when these drop from the sky, it's what's for dinner. Photo: U.S. Forest Service, USDA.

Adult pandora moth. Photo: U.S. Forest Service, USDA, by Terry Spivey.

east. Modern conflicts have arisen between the various Paiute tribes and the U.S. Forest Service, which wanted to spray to control the insect, as it feeds on various pine trees and had caused serious defoliation in Oregon, California, and Arizona. Catharine Fowler, an anthropology professor at the University of Nevada, Reno, who described pandora moth caterpillars as "very good—like a scrambled egg omelet with mushrooms," once mediated a dispute between the Paiute and the Forest Service as to whether the caterpillars would be poisoned. That time the Paiute won.

The larvae are collected at their most mature stage, during their July migration to the forest floor at the end of their first year of life. They are gathered by hand once or twice a day and temporarily stored in trenches in the ground. The larvae are then roasted in fire-heated sand for 30 minutes; the sand not only cooks the insects but also removes the fine hairs. The cooked larvae are washed, sorted, and dried. Stored in a cool and dry place, they keep for at least a year. The dried *piuga* are reconstituted before consumption by boiling for about an hour in plain or salted water. The boiled larvae have an odor described as like that of cooked mushroom. They are finger food; the entire larva is eaten except for the head. The cooking water is also used as broth or as a base for a *piuga* stew with whatever vegetables are desired. Scientific investigators have concluded that the pandora moth provided a significantly greater nutrient return for effort expended than did plant resources.

ARMYWORMS (MILLER MOTHS)

The army cutworm (*Euxoa auxiliaris*) is a species of moth larva. Its nickname "miller moth" comes from the fine scales on its wings that rub off easily and remind folks of the dusty flour on a miller, thus the name. Its caterpillars are pests of oats and common wheat but are a superior foodstuff themselves.

The miller moth is a seasonal nuisance in the spring in states such as Colorado, New Mexico, and Kansas, where they hatch in the low-lying farmlands and then migrate to higher elevations for the summer. They return as the weather cools but in smaller numbers. They are considered nearly impossible to control through normal

The ubiquitous miller moth that bears, and cats under the porch light, eat. Human cognoscenti prefer the larvae. Photo: USDA, USFS via Wikipedia.

Banana and Worm Bread
Courtesy of Iowa State University Entomology Club

1 cup flour
1 teaspoon baking soda
I teaspoon salt
1/2 cup chopped nuts
2 eggs
1/4 cup dry-roasted armyworms
3/4 cup sugar
2 bananas, mashed (2 cups)

Mix together all ingredients. Bake in greased loaf pan at 350°F for about 1 hour.

pest extermination techniques because a new batch shows up every day as they migrate. With their very small bodies, they enter homes in the evening (attracted by the light) through any available crack or crevice (e.g., door jamb or chimney). Other than being a nuisance, they are not considered harmful. They travel to alpine regions in late June and early July, where they feed at night on wildflower nectar. Army cutworm moths are one of the richest foods for predators, such as brown bears, because up to 72 percent of the moth's body weight is fat, thus making it more calorie rich than elk or deer.

CORN BORERS

The European corn borer (*Ostrinia nubilalis*), also known as the European high-flyer, is a pest of grain, particularly corn. The insect is native to Europe, originally infesting varieties of millet, including broom corn. The European corn borer was first reported in North America in 1917 on the East Coast. Since its initial discovery in the

European corn borer. Photo: Jeff Delonge, © www.entomart.be.

European corn borer larva. Photo: Marvin E. Rice, USDA Research Service.

Corn Borer Muffins

Cornbread mix
3/4 cup dry-roasted corn borers

Prepare batter according to instructions. Stir in grubs. Bake. Corn borers taste like—yep, you guessed it—corn.

Americas, it has spread north to Canada and westward to the Rocky Mountains. European corn borer caterpillars damage the ears of corn, as well as the stalks, by chewing tunnels, which cause the plants to fall over.

TOMATO HORNWORMS AND TOBACCO HORNWORMS

These two are closely related, but tomato hornworms have eight V-shaped markings while tobacco hornworms have seven diagonal lines. They both feed on plants of the family Solanaceae, commonly attacking tomato, eggplant, pepper, tobacco, moonflowers, and potato. It is not uncommon to find both eating on the same plant. Because, as noted elsewhere, some insects collect toxins—from metals to plant chemicals—they should not be eaten if picked from a tobacco plant. Also, since all plants in this family contain solanine, it might be wise to purge these worms before cooking them in oil, although they are listed in various publications as edible.

These are but one species of sphinx moth caterpillars, among several native to North and Central America, and they are all similar in appearance, as are they in the adult moth stage. Native Americans in California sought out caterpillars of the white-lined sphinx moth,

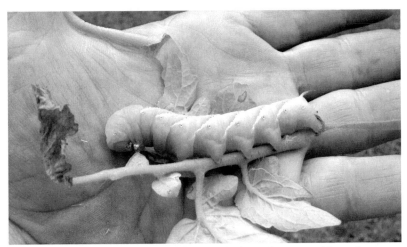

Voracious but succulent, tomato hornworm and tobacco hornworm (shown here on a tomato leaf) grow to considerable size. Photo: George Bredehoft, via Wikipedia.

in particular. These various caterpillars of the sphinx moth family are worthy prey because of their size, and are easily identified by their horn-like tail. Larger caterpillars, of all species and in all locations, are often cleaned quite efficiently by laying them across the palm, grasping the head between the thumb and forefinger, and with a motion like milking a cow or goat, "milking" the contents of the intestinal cavity out the back end: quick, simple, efficient, and messy if you don't watch where you aim. This also removes problems with what the caterpillar may have eaten. They still should be cooked, however. Most such caterpillars taste best when fully mature, as they are storing fat.

GRASSHOPPERS (LOCUSTS), CRICKETS, AND KATYDIDS
(Order Orthoptera)

Grasshoppers and crickets and their relatives have played an important role in the history of human nutrition. Because they are universally distributed and easy to catch, they are among the most common insects used for human food. Roasting and sautéing are frequently used methods of cooking, after first removing the wings and small legs. Because they have a mild flavor, they adapt well to local preferences for seasoning. Seasonings such as onion, garlic, cayenne, hot pepper, or soy sauce may be added. Candied grasshoppers, known as *inago*, are a favorite cocktail snack in Japan.

Locusts are the swarming phase of short-horned grasshoppers of the family Acrididae. These are species that can breed rapidly under suitable conditions and subsequently become gregarious (i.e., living in flocks) and migratory. They form bands as nymphs and swarms as adults—both of which can travel great distances as a plague, laying waste to the countryside like Sherman through Georgia.

GRASSHOPPERS

Among grasshoppers, there are 10 families, and these represent about 60 percent of the edible resource among Orthoptera worldwide. Grasshoppers are the most-eaten type of insect because of their wide distribution, many and diverse species, and the ease of harvesting them. They come in all colors, often having to do with their habitat, from green to brown to gray to pink and yellow and all shades in between. Most turn an attractive red when they are boiled or fried, which has led to their being promoted in Thailand as "sky prawns."

As kids in the Pacific Northwest, we would chase the big three-inch grasshoppers that had a noisy clacking flight; remove their legs, wings, and head; and boil them in pumpkin pie spice like we did crawdads. They have a mild flavor that takes seasoning well and are good wilderness fare simply roasted over a fire. We dressed them the same way, boiled them in salt water, and strung them in garlands in the smokehouse when we were smoking smelt, and they were delicious. Once crunchy dry, they kept for a year in a sealed jar.

Although grasshoppers were used extensively as food by Native American tribes in western North America, little is known about which species were preferred—if there was a preference. A small-scale way of harvesting the insects was for a number of people to form a large circle around a large bed of coals and then drive them toward the fire, where at least some would lose their wings, drop, and be roasted. As there are usually several species of range grasshoppers present at any one time and location, probably any roasted grasshopper was fair game.

Missionaries of the 1800s recorded that one mass-harvest technique common to several tribes was a simple drive. They'd dig a pit 10–12 feet in diameter and 4–5 feet deep in the center of a 4–5 acre field. Surrounding the field with men with long brush beaters, they'd drive the grasshoppers to the center, where they fell into the pit. Often, a 3–4 acre drive would fill such a hole. A variation of this, similar to the small-scale harvest above, was to build a light brush fire covering 20 to 30 square feet. The people then formed a large circle around it and drove the grasshoppers onto the hot coals. Sometimes a field was simply set afire, and the scorched grasshoppers were picked up afterward. Or, as in the case of Mormon crickets, grasshoppers could be collected by hand in the early morning, when they were too cold to be active. Pulverized grasshoppers were often mixed with serviceberries and hard-dried for a long-lasting pemmican—a trade good staple among various tribes.

Spring 1985 saw uncountable numbers of the migratory grasshopper *Melanoplus sanguinipes* wash up on the eastern shore of the Great Salt Lake in Utah. Researcher Dave Madsen noted that "neat rows of salted and sun-dried grasshoppers stretched for miles along the beach," with the widest rows ranging up to more than six

There are some 11,000 species of grasshoppers. Many are in the color of their environs, and they come in all sizes. They are eaten worldwide and have been for ages. Photo: Stephen Friedt, via Wikipedia.

feet in width and nine inches deep and containing up to 10,000 grasshoppers per foot. Madsen's team found that one person could collect some 200 pounds an hour, or 273,000 calories per hour of work: deer or antelope, assuming a successful hunt, return about 25,000 calories per hour of work invested. The team subsequently found nearby caves where natives had come to harvest and winnow the sand from these ready-made, seasonal delicacies, and according to the coprolite in the caves, they snacked as they worked.

Although a worldwide staple, grasshoppers, in particular, can carry several parasitic worms that can be passed to humans, so roasting or boiling is important for more than taste—just as with store-bought eggs and chicken. In a domestic setting, grasshoppers are often captured and kept for a day to purge before being dressed and prepared, but they still must be cooked.

When grasshoppers swarm as locusts, it's hard not to catch them. One or two are most easily captured when they sit quietly, relying on their camouflage, or are distracted. Don't worry about being polite: they'll die happy, and you'll have lunch. These desert locusts were photographed on the Red Sea coast. Photo: Christiaan Kooyman, via Wikipedia.

Because of their mild taste that goes with any seasoning, and because of their wide use as food, recipes abound. Most start with fresh insects that have been boiled and dressed, or dried/roasted stock reconstituted by boiling. One of the easiest recipes is to dip them in egg and then corn flour and fry them in oil. Drained, they make good finger food with many dips or, with a nod to John the Baptist, dipped in honey.

If your tastes run to Tex-Mex cooking, try this: get about a thousand small grasshoppers, soak in clean water for 24 hours, and then boil and dry. Remove legs, wings, and heads, and fry with minced garlic, onion, salt, and lemon. Roll up in tortillas with chili sauce and guacamole. Serves six stalwarts, or about double that number of dilettantes. Among the favorite seasonings for grasshoppers is plain soy sauce or sweet-and-sour sauces with soy.

CRICKETS

True crickets are one of the few Orthoptera that are both harvested and raised for food. Crickets may be easier to catch than single grasshoppers, as they usually hang out in dark, moist places under things, where they find their food. They are most commonly served fried, with picante, soy-based, or sweet sauces. They are sold dried and candied in the Far East. Yes, lots of folks eat 'em raw in Central America . . . but they also drink the water.

Typical of the some 900 species of crickets, this Gryllus has the classic shape. Most crickets are either black or dark brown and tend to be omnivorous. Photo: Roberto Zanon, via Wikipedia.

KATYDIDS (MORMAN CRICKETS)

The Mormon cricket, *Anabrus simplex* (Orthoptera: Tettigoniidae), was an important insect food of native tribes all over the West. Despite its moniker, the Mormon cricket is actually a shield-backed katydid. (Katydids lay eggs on plants; grasshoppers lay them in the

Growing to nearly three inches long, the Mormon cricket can be a food source or food pest, depending on whether you are growing or harvesting. Although flightless, they can travel a mile and a half a day. Photo: Utah Camera, via Wikipedia.

ground.) It is a large insect, about two inches in length and wingless, and it travels in large, dense bands. Bands may be more than a mile wide and several miles long, and with 20 to 30 or more crickets per square yard. It is sometimes damaging to crops or range vegetation and has been a pest target of the U.S. Department of Agriculture since before the turn of the century.

A favorite way to use these crickets was in a dark bread. The katydids were dried and then ground into flour on the same mill used to grind pine nuts or grass seed. The flour kept a long time, if stored dry. The crickets made the bread sweet.

There were several efficient methods of harvesting Mormon crickets, such as driving them into a stream and catching them by the bushel in large baskets. They were also simply scooped up from under vegetation when they were too cold to move. Native American

Resembling grasshoppers, most katydids are green, and some even mimic leaves. Photo: Wikipedia.

women went out early in the morning and caught them, were back by sunrise, and spent the rest of the day roasting, drying, and pounding them and putting them in bags to be cached for the winter. Some pioneers reported that Mormon cricket soup tasted rather like venison. Grasshopper recipes also work well with Mormon crickets.

Dave Madsen, an archaeologist for the State of Utah, investigated the rate of return in collecting Mormon crickets as food. Crickets were collected from bushes, grass, etc., at an average of 2 1/3 pounds per hour. At 1,270 calories per pound, that's 2,959 calories an hour. Where they were concentrated, as along a stream they wanted to cross, they were collected at rates of 23,479 calories an hour. This compares very favorably with large game—which you may or may not catch and is more difficult to preserve.

In an article for *Natural History*, Madsen put cricket collecting in a contemporary context, noting that "one person collecting crickets from the water margin for one hour, yielding 18 1/2 pounds, therefore, accomplishes as much as one collecting 87 chili dogs, 49 slices of pizza, or 43 Big Macs." He concluded, "Our findings thus showed that the use of insects as a food resource made a great deal of economic sense."

CICADAS AND APHIDS
(Order Homoptera)

The Homoptera suborder includes many insects, such as aphids and leafhoppers, which are significant agricultural pests, but only the cicadas are used widely as human food, the aphids for treats. The nymphs of some species, known as "periodical cicadas," spend up to 17 years underground, where they feed on roots. After 17 years they emerge from the soil, climb up a tree trunk or fence post, and molt to the adult stage. Periodical cicadas (a complex of six species in the United States) occur as "broods," which appear above ground only once every several years in any one locality. When they do appear, however, it is often in vast numbers. They are delicious when fried or roasted to a golden brown. Many cicadas have shorter life cycles, and Indian tribes collected some of them as food in what is now the western United States. They are regularly eaten in many other countries, especially in Asia. Some are quite large.

As we go to press with this volume, North America is in the throes of another cicada emergence, and there are news stories here and there that "you know, you can [wink, wink, nudge, nudge] eat them," and from the more enlightened members of the Fourth Estate, the occasional recipe or two. Maybe if there were more diverse starting points for the various cycles among the nonannual species, we'd have an emergence every year, and folks could look forward to it like the annual smelt or salmon run, or waterfowl migrations.

When the cicadas come, gourmets (read that *cognoscenti*) thereof appear in the local paper with favorite recipes. These stories usually appear in the "local color" pages with pictures of an unwashed chef and not the cooking-and-recipe section, but try some of the following.

During the 2007 emergence, the delicious, plentiful cicada did a lot to promote the cause of entomophagy. Photo: Mariano Szklanny, via Wikipedia.

- Marinate cicadas in Worcestershire sauce for one hour. Dip in egg and then dredge in flour or breadcrumbs. Deep-fry and serve with soy or cocktail sauce.
- Place cicadas on a cookie sheet and roast for 10 to 15 minutes at 225 degrees. When dry, grind coarsely and use as a nut substitute in bread or on ice cream. A finer grind can be mixed 50/50 with flour to make high-protein dough.
- Drop cicadas briefly in boiling water. Coat with red pepper, garlic, and ground bay leaf.
- Stir-fry with garlic, ginger, and diced vegetables, with a little soy sauce.

Female annual cicada photographed in Winfield, Illinois. These cicadas also emerge all at once so they have a chance against predators—but only a year's worth at a time. Photo: Bruce Marlin, via Wikipedia.

Newly hatched cicadas, called tenerals, are the premium for eating because their shells are still soft. On older ones, I like to remove the wings and legs, as on grasshoppers and other insects.

APHIDS AND SUGAR

You probably learned in fifth-grade science class that ants farm (as in, herd and protect) aphids, and "milk" them. True, but that's only half the story. Ants take care of aphids and relieve them of their product, which the ants store. But where there are no ants, aphids produce a sweet "honeydew" secretion anyway, which builds up on the plant host. The mealy plum aphid, *Hyalopterus pruni*, winters over on various *Prunus* trees, but in April, May, and June it moves to the leaves of various aquatic plants, such as cattail, tule reeds, and

Above: There are myriad variations in the aphid family, distributed world-wide. Virtually all but the Native Americans have regarded them as an insufferable pest. Here a pea aphid tends her young; ants in turn tend aphids and extract their sugars. So can you. Photo: Shipher Wu, courtesy PLoS Biology and Wikipedia.

Right: Many aphids, such as this invasive Russian wheat aphid, congregate on grasses and sedges, where they and their sweet excretions can be readily harvested by stripping or shaking. Photo: USDA.

phragmites (reed "grass"). There they suck juices, which they convert to sometimes very heavy deposits of sugar. Missionaries in 1702 noted it had "all the sweetness of sugar." In 1841, explorers noted the natives would wipe the secretions, aphids and all, from the reed stems, press them into fist-sized balls, with a resulting look like "wet bran," which they dried, wrapped in leaves, and saved for later. The explorers loved the food, until they realized it was mostly aphids. Various natives would also gather the reeds early in the morning, dry them in the sun, and beat the dry sugar off onto skins to save it. Gathering of the honeydew was an annual seasonal activity of Indians of the Great Basin. Keeping in mind that sugar cane is a grass, you will not be surprised to find this product, with or without the aphids, tastes just like store-bought sugar.

ANTS, BEES, AND WASPS
(Order Hymenoptera)

Ants, bees, and wasps are social insects that undergo complete metamorphosis, which concentrates the supply for you. With bees and wasps, it is usually the bee or wasp "brood" (larvae/pupae) that is eaten. Adult bees and wasps don't taste good to most people, but among those who favor their flavor, "nutty" is usually the common description. Canned wasps, wings and all, are sold in Japan, and rice cooked with these wasps was a favorite dish of the late Emperor Hirohito.

With ants, it is also the larvae and/or pupae that are usually eaten, but not always. Roasted leafcutter ant abdomens are sold, instead of popcorn, in movie theaters in Colombia, South America. In some cultures, bee nests are collected as much for their bee grubs as for the honey. In Mexico, certain kinds of ant pupae, known as *escamoles,* are found on the menu in the finest restaurants. They are served fried with butter, or fried with onions and garlic.

ANTS

Some of the easiest ant nests to raid are the mound-building ant species in the genus *Formica*. They are known for their spraying of formic acid as a defense mechanism, and large

Knocking apart downed logs in the deep woods may expose nurseries filled with carpenter ant eggs or pupae. Not all ants are good food: various red ants usually aren't worth the fight, and fire ants are toxic and can poison fish. Photo: Muhammad Mahdi Karim, via Wikipedia.

```
┌─────────────────────────────────────────────────────────────┐
│                    Tex-Mex Ant Taco                          │
│                                                              │
│  1/2 pound (2 cups) ant larvae and pupae                     │
│  Butter                                                      │
│  3 serrano chilies, chopped                                  │
│  1 tomato, chopped                                           │
│  Handful of cilantro                                         │
│  1 taco shell                                                │
│  Seasonings                                                  │
│                                                              │
│  Fry the ant larvae and pupae in butter. Add the chilies,    │
│  tomato, and cilantro and stir. Add salt, pepper, cumin, or  │
│  oregano to taste, and place in taco shell.                  │
└─────────────────────────────────────────────────────────────┘
```

nests often can be located by the characteristic odor. These ants are too sour to be edible per se but are often used as seasoning in lieu of vinegar or lemon juice. However, the pupae do not have this strong, sour taste.

These ant workers take very good care of their young. The smallest larvae are kept in moist areas of the mound, but pupae need dry-warm conditions and are kept separate from the rest of the brood, and soon after the sun hits the mound they are moved toward the surface. The pupae can be collected just under the surface of the mound at that point, but know that they will later be moved back deeper if the sun gets too hot.

Black carpenter ant broods are often found by kicking apart rotten logs, and these are usually fair sized. Ground-dwelling ants are seldom worth the effort.

Boiled, ants can substitute for rice in most recipes. In the bush with no utensils, they can be roasted in hot sand.

BEES

Collecting honey from wild bee colonies is one of the most ancient human activities and is still practiced by aboriginals and country folk everywhere. Some of the earliest portrayals of gathering honey is shown in rock paintings dating to around 11,000 B.C. Gathering honey is usually done by subduing the bees with smoke and breaking open the tree or rocks where the colony is located, often resulting in the physical destruction of the nest location—and, in my experience, certain hazard to the robber.

Smoke calms bees; it initiates a feeding response in anticipation of possible hive abandonment due to fire, and smoke also masks alarm pheromones released by guard bees or when bees are squashed in an inspection. The ensuing confusion creates an opportunity for the beekeeper to open the hive and work without triggering a defensive reaction—*most of the time*. Because of Africanized bees, harvesting wild honey in the warmer regions of North America has become a hazardous proposition. A beehive, however, contains honey, bee bread (stored pollen), and brood—all nutritious.

Bees in a natural hive, located at Coromandel Valley, South Australia. Comb, brood, and bee bread (pollen) are all edible. Photo: Bilbyu, via Wikipedia.

Honeybees are widely eaten as well, after long-term boiling and then frying or sautéing, or dry-roasting and grinding. Although edible at all stages of growth, the immature stages are far more favored.

WASPS

When it comes to harvesting wasps, the book may not be worth the candle, with the exception of finding mud dauber (or dirt dauber) nests from which the young have not emerged. These multicompartmented adobe structures can be scraped or knocked from their mount, but you never know what you're getting: it could be only a wee egg and a drugged spider the mother wasp put in for food, or a mature one just about ready to fly when you disturbed it, or anything in between.

Wasps, hornets, bees, ants, and termites are social insects that conveniently congregate their broods for efficient harvesting by entomophagists. In some metropolitan venues, pickled wasps are a delicacy. Photo: Piccolo Namek, via Wikipedia.

Isolated small paper nests not enclosed in a large paper "house," but hung discreetly here and there, are also easy to knock down, as only a few adults usually guard them. I have read of natives knocking down and quickly knocking apart a large paper nest at night and then coming back to see if it has been abandoned, to harvest eggs and pupae. I have, however, seen large paper nests knocked apart on a fallen tree, which although apparently destroyed, were definitely not abandoned.

Others have reported a peanut-like flavor to wasps, but this writer would only favor their musty taste after he had eaten all the tree bark and grass in the area. I have read of Asians using smoke to drive adult wasps out of a paper nest, including the succulent queen, so they could raid the pupae, but it didn't work very well for us: they came boiling out of the nest, of course, but escape was not what they had on their minds.

TERMITES
(Order Isoptera)

Termites are most widely used as food in Africa, no doubt at least in part because the gigantic mounds (the termitaria, or mounds, of some species may be up to 20 feet high) make them easy to find, but they are one of the true luxury foods for a person in a survival situation anywhere they are found. Termites are social insects with colonies divided into "castes," which include workers, soldiers, winged adults, and a queen. Metamorphosis is incomplete. The queen becomes very large, and she lays thousands of eggs. Periodically, the winged adults emerge in huge swarms, mate while in flight, and then start new colonies.

All termites are delicious, but the soldiers carry a serious set of mandibles. Photo: Althepal, via Wikipedia.

Formosan termites, an invasive species, have become a real pest in North America. Eat lots of these swarmers (alates) and do everybody a favor. Photo: USDA.

Though all termites avoid the sun, they are highly attracted to lights, even candlelight, and that is one way they can be captured for use as food. The wings are broken off, and termites are delicious fried. Even Europeans eat them in Africa. The queens are considered a special treat and are often reserved for children or grandparents. There are considerable swarms in North America as well, but no nests as such, just individual colonies, so the best way to find termites and their brood is to knock apart their combination food/habitat of dead wood.

A common recipe for termites is to kill the mass in hot water and then sun dry and winnow away the wings (if alates) and legs. They can be "fried" in their own oil, seasoned with chilies, and served over rice. They all seem to have a roasted-nut flavor and are not unpalatable raw (but should be cooked if possible).

Because of their attraction to light as alates, some cultures put up nets around a lamp. The best harvest this writer ever made was when I kicked apart a log in the Pacific Northwest, which was full of alates evidently staging to swarm, and could be scooped up by the handful and later winnowed from the wood and leaf litter.

BEETLES
(Order Coleoptera)

Beetles are the most widely eaten type of insect: 344 species are known to be used as food. They are mostly eaten in the larval stage, although beetles have complete metamorphosis, and the larvae, pupae, and adults of many species are used as food. On adults, the hard parts (wings, legs, and head) are removed during preparation for cooking. The larvae (sometimes called "grubs") are soft-bodied, and are usually the best for food because of flavor and ease of preparation.

JUNE BUGS

Phyllophaga is a very large genus (more than 260 species) of New World scarab beetles in the subfamily Melolonthinae. Common names for this genus and many other related genera in the subfamily Melolonthinae are May beetles, June bugs, and June beetles. They range in size from a half inch to an inch and a half. Most are black-ish- or reddish-brown, without prominent markings, and often have a hairy belly. Nocturnal, they usually come to a light in numbers pro-portional to how many there are.

They may be stripped of all hard parts, boiled in salt water, and eaten, but the grubs are by far the best. The grubs should be soaked in saltwater overnight, squeezed from head to tail to empty the gut, and the head removed; cook the remaining carcass like shrimp. They even taste like shrimp, and the usual seasonings apply when avail-able. In the wild, they may be stripped, decapitated, and roasted on a stick inserted where the head was.

Above: A typical June bug, photographed in North Carolina. Photo: Patrick Coin, via Wikipedia.

Above right: June beetles in the larval stage are good too. These grubs are likely to be found in dense grass or turf, or the top layers of soil. Photo: Courtesy UGA.

Right: Ten-lined June beetle, common in the western United States. Photo: Calibas, via Wikipedia.

WESTERN CORN ROOTWORM

Diabrotica virgifera virgifera is one of the most devastating corn rootworm species in North America, especially in the Midwestern corn-growing areas, such as Iowa. A related species, the Northern corn rootworm, *D. barberi*, co-inhabits in much of the range and is fairly similar in biology.

The USDA estimates that corn rootworms cause $1 billion in lost revenue each year, which includes $800 million in yield loss and $200 million in cost of treatment for corn growers. The good news is, they taste pretty much like corn and are good eating as a beetle and not just as a grub.

Diabrotica virgifera virgifera. The adult stage of the western corn rootworm (shown searching for pollen on corn silk). Photo: USDA by Tom Hlavaty.

Rootworm Beetle Dip

2 cups low-fat cottage cheese
1 1/2 teaspoons lemon juice
2 tablespoons skim milk
1/2 cup reduced-calorie mayonnaise
1 tablespoon chopped parsley
1 tablespoon chopped onion
1 1/2 teaspoons fresh chopped dill weed
1 1/2 teaspoons beau monde or similar seasoning salt
1 cup dry-roasted (crushed, depending on the culinary client) rootworm beetles.

Blend cottage cheese, lemon juice, and milk. Stir in mayonnaise, parsley, dill, beau monde, and beetles. Chill and serve with corn chips.

GIANT WATER BUG
(Order Hemiptera)

The giant water bug *(Belostomatidae)* is well named. First, it is one of the few insects that is a true "bug" (as defined by having mouth parts adapted to piercing and sucking but not for chewing), and it is indeed a giant: up to 5 inches long in the species *Lethocerus americanus*, as found in slow-moving waters in Montana and Florida. The nicknames are appropriate as well: "alligator tick," "toe biter," and "electric light bug."

Until I watched my bud catch one in Montana, I had always thought the ones in *Indiana Jones* were stage props. They are the largest insects in North America, although not all species get as big as *Lethocerus*. Their bite is extremely painful, but not of medical significance. They will attack baby turtles, small water snakes, fish, and toes of the unwary Huck Finn. If you find these, your hunting/gathering will be much simpler than gathering ant larvae, as they are substantial. They are known to play possum when captured, or to exude fluid from their anus, and then to bite the hand that wants to feed on them: handle them from the sides, as you would a crayfish. Air breathers, they can be attracted to lights at water's edge.

See the photo on the next page, so you know we didn't make this one up.

The preferred method of cooking is boiling. In Asia they are often served with a ginger-flavored sauce, and they are also ground up with fish sauce, sugar, peppers, and shallots to make a sauce for rice or other foods. The one I tried—just served with salt, pepper, and lemon—had an earthy flavor, like small-pond bass.

Captured and photographed near Billings, Montana, this giant water bug may not look like lunch, but it is. Photo: Ken Aycock, via Wikipedia.

"AMERICAN" COCKROACH
(Order Blattaria)

Introduced to this continent from Africa in the early 1600s, the "American" cockroach has made itself at home anywhere it can stay warm and has a place to hide. Being flat-bodied, they can hide almost anywhere. There is not much of biological origin they will not eat.

Although I may be more broad-minded than some—after all, I'm trying to convince you to eat bugs—I have to admit a distaste for eating cockroaches. The ones I ate were lab-raised and heavily spiced, but I had a problem with the last ones I had seen "in the wild." Although they are shown to be not quite as high in protein as some insects, as insects go, they are OK human food from the standpoint of nutrition. My not having them on my short list of edibles has only to do with where they will live, and as a result the

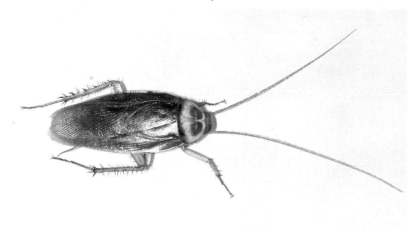

"American" cockroach. Photo: Gary Albert, via Wikipedia

potential diseases they carry. Their totally omnivorous diet draws them to various unwholesome environs, where they are almost sure to pick up human pathogens.

As a practical matter, they are one of the fastest insects on foot, making them impossible to catch by hand (although relatively easy to trap). Also as a practical matter, they have a distasteful (to some, but after all this *is* a cockroach) wax that can be removed by simmering in an acidic bath (vinegar or lemon juice). But if they are all you have, cook them thoroughly before you remove the head, wings, and legs. To remove these parts before cooking would certainly expose your hands to any pathogenic microbes they may carry.

WOODLICE
(Order Isopoda)

Sometimes referred to as "armadillo bugs," woodlice are crustaceans with a rigid shell or exoskeleton. The two related species, "pill bug" and "sow bug," are found almost exclusively in moist settings, under rocks, logs, or leaf litter, or behind dead bark on trees—always out of the light and sun. The pill bug (aka roly-poly) rolls into a ball as a defense mechanism, while the sow bug usually just tries to scurry away, but they're not very good at it and are easy to catch. Some sow bugs also have a bad odor or taste, which functions as a defense mechanism.

The preferred meal, the pill bug, *Armadillidium vulgare*, originated in Europe but has adapted well to North America. Because these two related animals like the same habitat and diet, they are often found together but do not interact. Worldwide, there are more than 3,000 species of both marine and land types, and they tend to be parasite free. They're all isopods, land-dwelling crustaceans that are relatives of lobsters, shrimp, and crabs. The pill bug is often called "land shrimp." Both the pill bug and sow bug breathe through gills, and because of those gills, these isopods need moist environs.

They are commonly boiled but are always crunchy because their shell is calcium based. Pill bugs are readily collected, as when disturbed they stop running and go into a ball that is easily picked up. In areas where they can thrive, they are found by the thousands. In his book *Why Not Insects?*, in 1885 Vincent Holt spoke highly of pill bugs:

> *I have eaten these, and found that, when chewed, a flavour is developed remarkably akin to that so much appreciated in their sea cousins. Wood-louse sauce is equal, if not distinctly superior to, shrimp . . . Collect a quantity of*

the finest wood-lice to be found (no difficult task, as they swarm under the bark of every rotten tree) and drop them into boiling water which will kill them instantly, but not turn red, as might be expected. At the same time put into a saucepan a quarter of a pound fresh butter, a teaspoonful of four, a small glass of water, a little milk, some pepper and salt, and place it on the stove. As soon as the sauce is thick, take it off and put in the wood-lice. This is an excellent sauce for fish. Try it.

A nearly ubiquitous North American immigrant found wherever there is shade, moisture, and dead vegetation, the pill bug is often called "land shrimp" both because of family relationship and taste. Photo: Franco Folini, via Wikipedia.

Culinary poor cousins of the pill bug, sow bug varieties are not universally tasty: some have a bad odor or taste. If you can, leave those for the chickens and go for the pill bugs. Photo: Botaurus-stellaris, via Wikipedia.

For haute cuisine, pill bugs are fed boiled potato for a few days; in the woods, boil them up and they're good to go. They taste enough like shrimp that they will interchange for culinary purposes, as far as flavor is concerned. The crunch may take some acclimatization.

Pill bugs are an excellent survival food because they are widely distributed, easily identified and harvested, pleasantly flavored, and nutritious. If your interest in crustaceans extends beyond their being a dinner date, read up on pill bugs: they're fascinating.

DESERT CENTIPEDE
(Order Scolopendromorpha)

Having been used to the busy little two-inchers I'd find in the compost pile, I was impressed when I met my first Sonoran giant (*Scolopendra heros*) centipede. It would take a lot of the little varieties to make a handful, but these seven-inch desert dwellers have more meat on them than a small crayfish, and they're quite a bit slower than the small varieties. Like all centipedes, they avoid the sun and like it moist but seem to survive well in the hard desert under rocks and logs; some authorities state they will also burrow.

Published recipes recommend a sweet and sour sauce; the ones I've dealt with I just whacked with sticks, cut off the head and biting

All centipedes are edible, but the giant desert variety is worth the effort. Their coloring varies. Photo: Matt Reinbold, via Wikipedia.

parts (actually modified front legs), roasted in the fire, and ate with bottled barbecue sauce. Crunchy but good. The smaller ones are too small to "bite" successfully, but they do try to bite when picked up. The ones in the woods generally are red-brown; the ones in the desert vary from pale amber to red-brown and translucent, like a scorpion's belly.

Note: Do not confuse centipedes with millipedes. Centipedes are flat, have fewer and larger legs, and are usually some shade of translucent red-brown. They have a poisonous bite but are edible. Millipedes are round, not flat; have many more, smaller legs; and most will roll up if bothered. They do not have a poisonous bite, but most carry cyanogens that make them poisonous to eat. They have a distinct, unpleasant odor.

DRAGONFLY
(COMMON GREEN DARNER)
(Order Odonata)

Dragonflies are some of the fastest and most maneuverable insects on the planet. They are total predators and very efficient at it, from whence the name. You will starve to death trying to catch them by hand even in a net, although people in Southeast Asia have gotten very good at it. Your best chance is to catch them sleeping on the underside of leaves along the water they frequent. They are soporific and catchable at night if you have a light. To cook, remove wings, head, and legs, and then roast. In Asia they are usually stir-fried with vegetables.

One of the largest dragonflies, the green darner is named for its resemblance to a darning needle. Found all over North America near water, it is the official insect of Washington State. Photo: Chuck Evans (Mcevan), via Wikipedia.

SHORE FLIES
(Order Diptera)

In the insect world, even something small can be a big food source if there are enough of them. Ask any trout springing into the air after a mayfly. There is a small fly (*Hydropyrus hians*) of the group called "shore flies" (*Diptera: Ephydridae*) that used to breed in prodigious numbers in the alkaline waters of Mono Lake and other alkaline lakes in eastern California and Nevada. The fly pupae washed ashore in long windrows, sometimes making a deposit two feet deep at the edge of the lake.

Ephydridae, typical of the some 1,500 species of shore fly. Photo: Christian Bier, via Wikipedia.

The Piaute and other tribes dried them in the sun and mixed them with acorns, berries, grass seeds, and other edibles to make a pemmican or bread. They are also eaten in their natural condition, frying them in their own oil, and reportedly tasting like pork cracklings. Early explorers estimated that hundreds of thousands of tons of these would wash ashore, gathered by "hundreds of bushels" by tribes who traveled considerable distances to harvest them. They were usually sun-dried, the shell rubbed off, and the remaining yellow kernel saved as an important staple.

One explorer recorded, "The Indians gave me some; it does not taste bad, and if one were ignorant of its origin, it would make fine soup. Gulls, ducks, snipe, frogs, and Indians fatten on it." Indeed, the difference between plague and plenty depends on whether you like the taste.

HOUSEFLIES
(Order Diptera)

Common flies are edible, including the "housefly" (*Musca domestica*) and various species of "carrion fly"—aka bluebottle or blowfly (Calliphoridae), of which there are some 1,100 types. But better let Mikey try 'em. Politicians and other maggots can be separated from the carrion, feces, open sores, or vomitus upon which they feed by using light to chase them into dark containers, but the house-

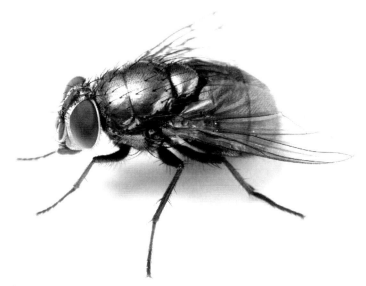

So foreign is the diet of a fly to the diet of man, and so disgusting is its status as a vector of human disease, it is easy to reject flies as a food source unless we first strain them through a chicken. Flies per se and fly maggots have the potential to be very nutritious, but they must be cooked to the point of sterilization. Photo: Antagain/iStock.

fly alone carries more than 100 human pathogens, most of which can be killers. Even with facilities to boil the maggot into sterility, in a "survival" situation there is probably no way to separate the maggots from their own feedstock without getting contaminated with whatever killed what they are eating, which even includes road kill, as sick animals get hit more often. By dry weight, house fly maggots are more than 50 percent protein. And you know what? I don't care.

SPIDERS AND SCORPIONS
(Arachnids)

Although not technically insects, I have included spiders and scorpions as "bug" food because they are treated much the same way as insects. I have sampled spiders, raw, and can report the one I tried was sweet and not unpleasant. Cooked tarantula spiders are considered a delicacy in Cambodia and by the Piaroa Indians of southern Venezuela, once they are singed of their body hair, but as a food source, gathering a quantity may be a consideration.

There are some 43,000-plus species of spiders classified so far. Almost all are edible, and almost all look like a spider. In North America the two dangerous species are the brown recluse "violin" spider (has a violin pattern on thorax) and the black widow (has orange hourglass shape on abdomen). Larger species such as the tarantula or "bird spider" of the Southwest deserts are most practical as food. This is a red-kneed Mexican tarantula. Photo: Trisha M. Shears, via Wikipedia.

This bark scorpion is from the Grand Canyon. Those species found in the Sonoran Desert are usually lighter to transparent. There are more than 1,700 species of scorpion worldwide, all are venomous, and most are potentially dangerous to man—but all are edible and in many venues are considered a delicacy. Photo: National Park Service.

Roasted scorpions are a common Chinese novelty food. I have tried scorpions but once and would have to be hungry to do so again. Some in the Sonoran Desert rival small crawdads in size—if not in succulence. We found them disconcertingly crunchy. To eat scorpions, except as a novelty, remove any hard parts as well as the tail.

MICROBES, TOXINS, OR ALLERGENS

Just as many plants and berries are poison; just as fowl, eggs, and pork must be cooked properly; and just as some people have deadly allergies to shellfish or tree nuts, some insects are poison, most should be cooked, many can become contaminated, and not all people can eat them.

As a sweeping generality, most insects, larvae, and mollusks should be cooked because they can carry parasites that transfer to man, and some serve as vectors for human diseases. Like us, insects are what they eat, and many eat toxic plants to which they have developed immunity, and store the toxins as a defense against predators. Some are toxic in their own right. Many of these are brightly colored as a warning ("aposematic"): bright colors (frequently black, red, yellow, orange, or marked with various combinations of these colors) and conspicuous behavior, such as leisurely flight, are generally indicative of chemical protection.

Some insects are subject to bioaccumulation of toxic metals. Thus, it is always good to know where your insect meal has been and what it ate. Although there are some 1,400-plus classified edible insects, I have cataloged only those that are easy to identify and have a long record of human consumption. Most are also plentiful in their own venue and season.

If you have food allergies, especially to shellfish, you should be cautious until you know how your body will react to any new food. Insects may be a source of individual allergens by ingestion, contact, or inhalation. It is not uncommon for persons working in the agricultural industry to develop contact allergies after repeated exposure to certain fairly common insect contaminants, especially when ground or macerated. I have a good friend who would be killed by a handful of walnuts. I had a cousin who would choke up and die within minutes if he touched a rabbit or a horse. I get an asthmatic reaction from moth "feathers" (scales) but have no problem eating the grubs.

Allergies are a complex and often individual thing, so go slow in uncharted waters: this includes eating new things, such as insects. Man may have eaten them since the dawn of time, but they are new to you. Your momma told you to chew your food. Uncle Fred tells you when eating the members of the animal kingdom discussed here to always cook your food. *Bon appétit!*